DAVID E. JOHNSTON

ROMAN VILLAS

Fifth edition

SHIRE ARCHAEOLOGY

British Library Cataloguing in Publication Data:
Johnston, David E.
Roman villas. – 5th ed. – (Shire archaeology; 11)
1. Architecture, Roman – Great Britain
2. Architecture, Domestic – Great Britain – History
3. Great Britain – Antiquities, Roman
I. Title
936.2'04
ISBN 0 7478 0600 4.

Published in 2004 by
SHIRE PUBLICATIONS LTD
Cromwell House, Church Street, Princes Risborough,
Buckinghamshire HP27 9AA, UK.
(Website: www.shirebooks.co.uk)

Series Editor: James Dyer.

ISBN 0 7478 0600 4.

Number 11 in the Shire Archaeology series.

First published 1979. Second edition 1983. Third edition 1988.
Fourth edition 1994. Fifth edition 2004.

Printed in Malta by
Gutenberg Press Limited, Gudja Road, Tarxien PLA 19, Malta.

Contents

4

List of illustrations

Note: In the illustrations the letter 'H' indicates a hypocaust, 'M' a mosaic and 'T' a tessellated floor.

Preface

When the first edition of this book appeared in 1979 many of us thought that it really was possible to define a Roman villa. Today we are more cautious. The trouble with definitions is that they exclude anything that does not fit within them – and so it was with this book. Fishbourne, for instance, was thought of as a palace and was only reluctantly admitted. The equally interesting walled complex at Gatcombe was not.

This fifth edition widens the scope and admits that many important sites defy classification into neat categories. Nowadays we use the term 'romanitas' when discussing the Roman aspirations of an owner who might reasonably have called his cottage a 'villa'. This is why we start our evolution with a two-roomed cottage whose excavator does not even use the term 'villa' to describe it. At the other extreme, the terms 'villa' and 'site' are inadequate to describe somewhere as comprehensive as Stanwick, where a large swathe of Romanised landscape is under investigation as we write.

Definitions apart, this fifth edition offers more villas to visit (in chapter 10) and better directions for finding them. It is still unfortunately true that British villas are concentrated in the south of England. On the other hand, there is no excuse for neglecting those that we do have. Some villas are barely worth visiting, and below we point an accusing finger at the worst. That said, most of the villas in this book are well maintained and a source of pride to their owners.

In preparing the text and illustrations I have drawn heavily on the published and unpublished work of others, in many cases redrawing and interpreting. I am deeply grateful to those numerous friends and colleagues who have allowed me to do so and who have discussed their work with me. The value of this new edition, moreover, has been enhanced by the work of talented illustrators whose art is both instructive and a pleasure to look at. We have taken the opportunity in this edition to go into colour as well, and this has meant replacing many of the illustrations. I am deeply grateful to many colleagues who have allowed me to use their pictures, even anticipating their full publication in some cases. I hope that they and all copyright holders will find that their material has been correctly acknowledged.

My personal thanks must include Roy Friendship-Taylor, Tony Rook, David Neal, David Tomalin, Keith Jarvis and John Cull. In this edition in particular I have been indebted to my wife, Pamela, for doing all the driving, suggesting improvements to the text and saving me from numerous mistakes. Above all, I wish to thank the editorial team at Shire Publications, who have been unfailingly patient and courteous at all times.

1

Farm or villa?

In the landscape of Roman Britain the villas stand out as focal points. Most of that landscape was farmed – or at least managed – by native Britons. In their settlements, farms and villages the Britons could display the extent to which they had adopted the standards and way of life of the Roman world. In other words, it is the degree of *romanitas* that distinguishes a villa from a farm.

For the villa owners this *romanitas* was the passport to a new world of consumer goods, personal prestige and self-advancement. The new tastes were reflected in the mosaics, wall-paintings, dining-rooms and sumptuous baths that we all associate with the villas. The patrons were often the old aristocracy of pre-Roman Britain serving as councillors and magistrates in the cities. The new towns and cities had introduced a way of life that was impossible in pre-Roman Britain, and so we can think of the villas as taking the luxuries of town life into the countryside.

The other side of the picture is more mundane, but equally absorbing. It is of the villa as a farm, a food-producing machine. In archaeological terms we have to identify an estate, with forests, meadows and cultivated fields; we have to excavate grouped or scattered buildings that can range from cowsheds to corn-driers, from watermills to wine cellars. The estate produced, and to a large degree also processed, not only food but other animal products (leather, tallow and wool, for example) and the timber that was used in far greater quantities than today. So we occasionally find evidence for tanning and fulling, and a few villas were truly 'industrial', being attached to potteries and tile-kilns. Hunting, fowling and fishing were more than mere recreational pursuits; they were the proper exploitation of all the natural resources of a varied estate.

Not all villas were run for private profit, however. The small farmer could have been a tenant or bailiff of a landowner who might live as far away as North Africa and have property in many provinces, or he could have been a tenant of the emperor. We return to questions of tenure in later chapters. In times of civil war the estates of those on the losing side were confiscated by the state; in peacetime (though this is hard to establish) they were bought, sold or amalgamated. In the troubled times elsewhere of the third century AD there are signs that continental entrepreneurs were investing in property in Britain. By the end of the period inflation was running high and the financial burdens of civic office that landowning entailed were becoming insupportable. Only the

1. Bignor (West Sussex): Richard Smirke's drawing of the Venus Room in 1812 shows the partly collapsed hypocaust as it was found. (Trustees of Bignor Roman Villa)

largest estates could survive, with small farmers and peasants locked in a circle of debt and bondage that amounted almost to serfdom. The father's occupation was now legally binding on the son, and those who abandoned their work or property could be rounded up like slaves. This is the social background to some, at least, of the villas in this book.

We may be wrong to think of a single owner in every case. Current thinking suggests that there could have been two, three or more families to a villa. This certainly makes sense at Newton St Loe (Somerset) (figure 3), with two self-sufficient houses next to each other. As families grew and subdivided, so the ground plan became more complex. This must have happened at Bignor (West Sussex), with up to four units, and at Chedworth (Gloucestershire), where a duplicate suite of living- and dining-rooms, kitchen and baths was provided in the north wing.

We now know the names of several villa owners, but frustratingly

2. Cropmarks of a villa and a pre-Roman enclosure can be seen in this false-colour air photograph of Woodhams Farm, Kings Worthy (Hampshire): A, villa; B, 'banjo' enclosure; C, undated fields and a 'droveway'. (© Crown copyright. NMR)

little about them. Such are Firminus (Barnsley Park, Gloucestershire), Naevius (Combe Down, Bath), Tiberius Claudius Severus (Piddington, Northamptonshire) and Quintus Natalius Natalinus (Thruxton, Hampshire). A certain Faustinus owned a villa in Norfolk that we have yet to find; in

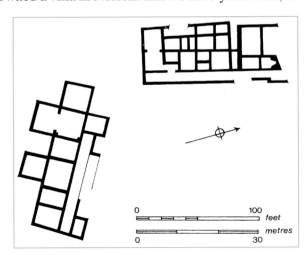

3. Newton St Loe (Somerset): adjacent family dwellings.

4. A portrait of the owner or his wife? A wall-painting from the baths at Sparsholt (Hampshire) was found in the fragments and was extensively restored by the late Dr Norman Davey. (Winchester City Museum)

5. Who owned the villa at Piddington (Northamptonshire)? Two different tile-stamps (specially made for the villa) may give us the names of two successive owners – Tiberius Claudius Severus and Tiberius Claudius Verus. (T. May and R. Friendship-Taylor)

6. Lullingstone (Kent): the villa as it may have looked in its heyday, *c.*AD 350. The dining-room is in the centre, with the baths on the extreme left. To the right, the sloping site is crowned by the temple-mausoleum and the grounds ran down to the riverside. (Graham Sumner)

figure 4 we may be looking at a portrait of an owner or his wife; and we would like to put life back into the young couple buried in the family mausoleum in the grounds of the Lullingstone villa in Kent (figure 6).

At Lullingstone we can at least trace the religious beliefs of successive owners (figure 7). In the second century part of the house was a shrine to three water goddesses (seen painted in a niche), while a later family converted the rooms above to a Christian house-church. Many villa owners were Christian – one, at Hinton St Mary (Dorset), boldly commissioning a mosaic floor showing the head of Christ and scenes of paradise (now in the British Museum). Others, however, were understandably ambiguous in their professions of faith. How far their employees followed suit we cannot say; who, for instance, carved the little Christian sign, possibly on the fountain or water shrine, at Chedworth? Ambiguity and secrecy were characteristic of the pagan 'mystery' religions, and the excavators suggested that the detached dining and reception complex of the excavated villa at Littlecote (Wiltshire) was the meeting place of such a cult. A less romantic view sees the building (which was unheated) merely as a summer dining-room. There are similarly cryptic mosaics in the villa at Brading (Isle of Wight).

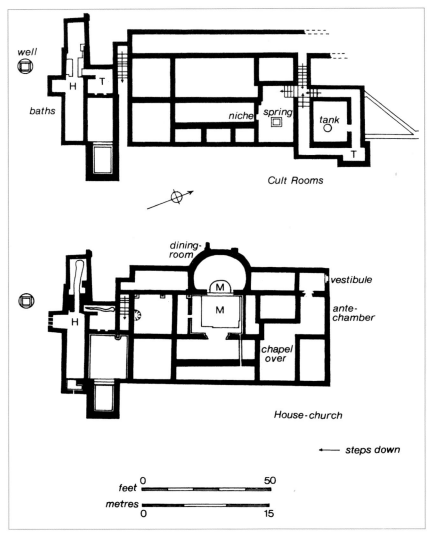

7. Lullingstone: (above) the evidence for a water cult in the second century; (below) fourth-century modifications in which part of the building became a self-contained Christian chapel.

8. Lullingstone: the chi-rho monogram, with the letters alpha and omega, which greeted worshippers to the chapel. (The British Museum)

Some villas seem to have been part of a much larger community or settlement. At Stanwick (Northamptonshire) a large area of 28 hectares (70 acres) or more that has been destined for gravel extraction was in 2004 being studied with this in mind (figure 10). This was not a villa 'estate' with clearly defined boundaries but rather a landscape of drove-roads, enclosures and villages that evolved in the first century BC and persisted through the Roman period. The luxurious Stanwick villa seems

9. The grandeur of a big villa is suggested by this painting of the main range at Littlecote (Wiltshire). Beyond, to the right, is a detached dining-room that might have been a cult centre. (Painting by L. Thompson, copyright Roman Research Trust, Littlecote)

to have had a satellite – perhaps a bailiff's office or administrative centre where, for instance, rents might have been paid. The paved courtyard was flanked impressively by towers and a formal entrance, but apparently the building was only thatched, sparsely furnished and utterly functional. Now if we visualise the main villa at Stanwick along with its satellite (the administrative centre) and with the modest winged corridor house some 1500 metres (1640 yards) away at Redlands Farm then we can comprehend a hierarchy that ranges from the country house to farmsteads and isolated habitations. Peculiarities in the archaeological record of other British sites suggest that the term 'villa' should embrace large rural communities of this kind. Nevertheless, at this stage in our thinking we cannot truly say that we understand the real nature of some of the larger establishments.

Finally we return to the economic significance of the villa. From the earliest years of the Roman occupation it was a functional response to new, heavy demands on the peasant farmer – the growing markets in the new towns, the requisitions for the army of occupation and, above all, the demands of the tax collector. Although life in the fields and villages may have looked much the same as it had for centuries, everyone felt the pressures of central government. This, then, is how the villas came into being, not only in Britain but in most of the western Empire: the adaptation of a Celtic way of life to the requirements of the classical world.

10. The landscape setting of the villa and associated buildings at Stanwick (Northamptonshire). The villa is seen to be one of many elements in the landscape. (From D. and P. Dark, after P. Salway and D. S. Neal)

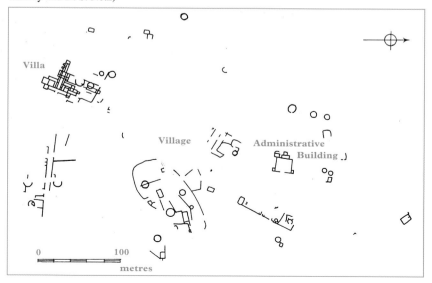

2

The simple house

The Roman occupation lasted nearly four hundred years – roughly as long as from the time of Queen Elizabeth I to the present day – and the changes over that period were equally profound. So we must expect the major villas, like any country house, to have evolved often unrecognisably from their simple beginnings. Some later examples emerged fully fledged from the drawing board, while a few remained as cottages, without elaboration; generally, however, we find a simple 'cottage-house' embedded in something more complex.

Figure 11 shows the most basic **cottage-house**, barely recognisable as a villa but constructed in the Roman period and showing some elements of *romanitas*. It was excavated at Ower (Dorset) and the experimental replica can be seen not far away at the Upton Country Park. The building might have been built and used by the nearby salt-workers, who were familiar with the roundhouses of the Iron Age. Its interesting shape ('a squashed round-house', according to its excavator) is a unique compromise between the circular prehistoric hut and the Roman house with a pitched roof. The materials used were not wattle

11. Upton Country Park (Dorset): a replica of the building excavated at Ower. This represents the most basic type of 'cottage-house' of the first century AD.

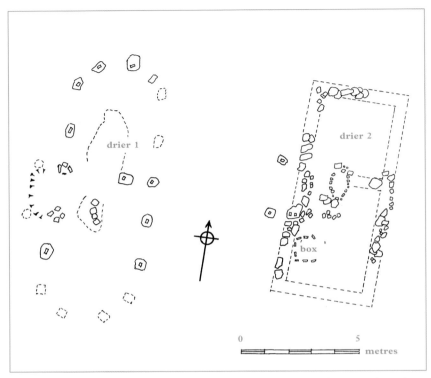

12. Ower (Dorset): the original of the building shown in figure 11. Of the two phases here, the first was chosen for replication.

and daub but cob (compacted chalk) and timber, and the walls were supported at ground level on a series of stone post-pads. There was a simple porch and the interior was dominated by a kiln or drier. The illustration also shows the final phase some years later. The post-pads have been replaced by stone walls, a curious 'box' has appeared and the whole structure has been refurbished to become more fashionably rectangular.

The next example, Lockleys, near Welwyn (Hertfordshire), is a classic case. Casual pre-Roman occupation is shown by a circular hut and other features. The first Roman house, of timber, was built between AD 50 and 120 and subsequently removed, leaving only a row of post-holes. The first stone-built house is a late example of a **strip-house** (about AD 300) that soon had two wings added, with a corridor or veranda in front, to look like figure 13. The slope of the ground allowed the luxury of an upper floor at the nearer end. The further modifications followed a fire

13. Lockleys (Hertfordshire): the villa as it may have looked in the fourth century AD. (After H. C. Lander)

in about AD 340. The resultant **winged-corridor plan** is also clearly seen at Park Street, St Albans (Hertfordshire) (figure 14), where a strip-house was similarly incorporated in the middle of the second century AD.

These modifications are very significant; the rectangular stone strip-houses show the impact of Rome on a Celtic land in which the circular hut was the normal house form. Subsequently the widespread adoption of the winged-corridor plan and veranda, with or without a porch, represents an architectural cliché that was universal throughout the Empire – the pillared, classical façade. This Mediterranean form may seem inappropriate in dark and windy Britain, but the veranda does admit a large amount of light. At Sparsholt (Hampshire) the veranda was evidently open to the elements, with evidence of weathering.

The winged-corridor plan marks an advance in other important ways. In the strip-house the rooms were probably interconnected, of equal importance and with little privacy. The corridor allowed a hierarchy of rooms, the separation of the head of the family and other members of the household, and a range of different uses for the rooms. Structurally, too, the changes were important; the roof structure was more complicated and less light reached the main rooms. Windows were therefore restricted to the open side, with either clerestory lights or dormers above the veranda. Consequently the main walls and the ceilings (if any) had to be taller, making the rooms more elegant and airy. Additional storage space was provided either by a ceiling with strong joists or by a clerestory that effectively added another storey.

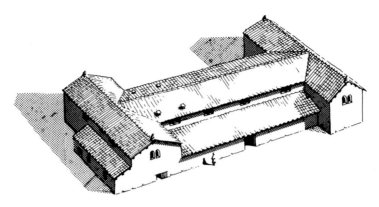

14. Park Street (Hertfordshire): (above) as it may have looked in the late second century, and (below) its final fourth-century form. (After N. Davey)

When a further range of rooms was provided at the back, giving the **tripartite corridor plan**, the problem of lighting must have been acute. This plan was adopted in the main house at Brading (Isle of Wight) and at Frocester Court (Gloucestershire) (figure 45). Another solution was to have wings fore and aft, as at Park Street. This would have allowed one wing to be used for welcoming visitors, or to serve as a farmyard, with the opposite wing as a garden. Finally, a **courtyard villa** can be described either as an arrangement of buildings grouped around a courtyard or as one in which the house itself has an internal courtyard. We return to these in our next chapter.

The roofs sometimes carried ventilators and chimney-pots. Fireplaces with hoods, to burn charcoal or coal, were occasionally fitted, as at Newport (Isle of Wight) (figure 15). Frequently fireplaces, hearths and hypocausts were vented under the eaves as if the roof itself were on fire.

On the whole the functions of individual rooms elude us, though we can sometimes guess in very simple cases, such as figure 16. Here we can imagine a quiet, private end (the 'study' was heated by a brazier), a fine central reception and dining-room with mosaic (accessible, admittedly, to livestock from the farmyard outside) and a warm but noisy end, with kitchen, servants' room (a 'squalid, smoky den' according to the excavator) and a room warmed by the gentle, steady heat of a channelled (not pillared) hypocaust. Bedrooms are hard to identify, though one room at Lullingstone (Kent) had two depressions in the floor, containing coins, each perhaps under the head of a mattress or narrow bed. Generally, however, the Roman couch (a day-bed, like a chaise-longue) was used for sleeping, and in a villa any living-room could serve as a bedroom. Kitchens were disappointingly unsophisticated, the principal feature being the hearth; this was a masonry block upon which a charcoal fire was lit. Above this was placed a portable gridiron on which pots could be simmered and meat grilled. Bathrooms were usually either detached (because of the fire risk) or placed at one end of the range. Lavatories are found in towns rather than in villas (perhaps because of the proximity of suitable tree cover) and domestic rubbish was disposed of in pits or out of the window (as at Sparsholt, where a

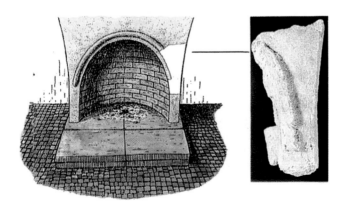

15. Newport (Isle of Wight): a reconstruction view of the wood-burning fireplace. (Inset) A fragment of the plaster moulding.

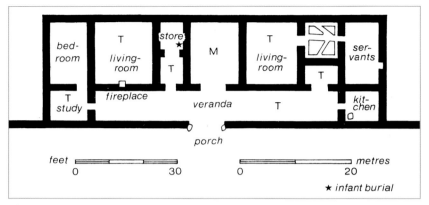

16. Sparsholt (Hampshire): the main house as originally built (the wings were *not* added later). The function of individual rooms is suggested. The infant burial may represent a dedication and indicate the family shrine. (Author)

midden accumulated among the nettles in an angle of the outside walls where nobody ever went). Excavators often encounter burials of newborn infants, either as a dedication (figure 16) or as the surreptitious evidence of unofficial births at the villa. There were ninety-seven at Hambleden (Buckinghamshire), where the farmyard 'was positively littered with babies' in the excavator's words. Finally, indoor shrines must have existed, but they or their contents are seldom recognised.

17. Sparsholt, as conjecturally restored. Note the contrasting use of brick and limestone tiles. The wooden veranda was definitely open to the elements.

3
The complex villa

It is often said that there was a second flowering of villas in the fourth century. Research has now shown that the number of villas reached a peak in about AD 325 but that the overall sizes of the villas decreased. In other words, the taste for building such luxuries was working its way down the social scale to those who felt they had 'arrived' and could afford a proper villa. The new estates were correspondingly small; evidently the display of affluence was more important than substantial agricultural productivity.

A garden (rather than a working farmyard) displayed that affluence to visitors on arrival. Good evidence for gardens is rare, so that from Frocester Court (Gloucestershire) (figure 18) is useful. Here a compact main house (which significantly evolved from a strip-house) had a fine display of ditched enclosures around a walled courtyard. There were two gardens; that behind the house had soil suitable for vegetables, while in front were formal flower-beds flanking the gravel drive with its turning area. These were omitted over an earlier cemetery that was left turfed, while a narrow hedge apparently screened an external stokehole from the view of visitors. The roses of Fishbourne (West Sussex) are well authenticated. On other sites, such as Chedworth (Gloucestershire) and Latimer (Buckinghamshire), we can make only an intelligent guess at the layout of flower-beds, hedges, trees and kitchen gardens.

18. Frocester Court (Gloucestershire): excavated evidence for the garden.

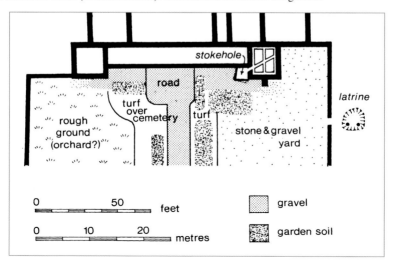

19. Cropmarks and field boundaries of the walled villa at Ditchley (Oxfordshire). (Ashmolean Museum)

The Ditchley villa (Oxfordshire) (figure 19) was clearly approached by a drive between paddocks or orchards. The courtyard wall at this villa enclosed a farmyard with a well (the dark spot) and a circular threshing-floor. Such a coherent layout usually evolved over a period, as at Sparsholt (Hampshire), where a lack of privacy in the aisled building is thought to have driven the owner to build his new house nearby, forming the beginning of a symmetrical courtyard (figure 54). The more complex sequence at Gadebridge Park (Hertfordshire) included the removal of the main yard from one side of the house to the other (figure 53). By now (early fourth century) the main attractions were the new heated rooms (under the tower-like wings of figure 28), the rebuilt bath suite and the large swimming-pool (an unusual feature). As the waters may have been curative, the villa could have functioned less as a farm than as a 'health farm' or private spa. The final phases of these two villas are discussed in chapter 8. The apparent disintegration of a unified house plan is seen in the final phase of Park Street (Hertfordshire) (figure 14), while a masterpiece of conversion is seen at Rapsley, Ewhurst (Surrey), in the left-hand building of figure 21. The architect has defied boggy and uneven ground to transform a compact orthodox bath-house by stages into a convincing winged-corridor dwelling-house.

Villas such as Chedworth, with a double courtyard, doubtless a farmyard and a private garden, display a deceptive unity. There is now little sign of the three original buildings sharing a common bath suite

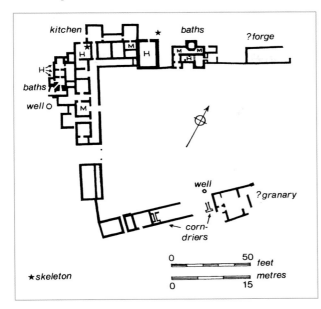

20. At Rockbourne (Hampshire) the family did not share their bath-house with the workers on the estate. Of the two burials shown, one skeleton was found in the hypocaust, evidently someone killed while robbing the masonry; the other was in a grave, presumably post-Roman. The scene before the hypocaust collapsed is shown in figure 58.

21. Rapsley, Ewhurst (Surrey), as it may have appeared about AD 280. (C. de la Nougerede)

22. Woodchester (Gloucestershire): this painting by Steve Smith gives a good idea of the size and complexity of this grandiose villa.

and water shrine; nor of the independent family unit apparently provided at the end of the north wing. The great establishment at Brading (Isle of Wight) (figure 52) was also probably in two parts, the better-known half consisting of a winged-corridor house flanked tidily by aisled buildings with others perhaps beyond. In the great villas of Gaul the main house frequently looked out over two rows of outbuildings (often not parallel but diverging to enhance the effect of distance). The intermediate phase at Bignor (West Sussex) was of this tapering, Gaulish plan. In its final form this unity has been abandoned; the private parts are completely secluded, although house and farmyard are enclosed by a single unifying wall. Rockbourne (Hampshire) (figures 20 and 68) is another large complex probably enclosing a farmyard and private garden and separate baths for family and estate workers. North Leigh (Oxfordshire) has two wings open to view, with the other two being easy to trace on the ground, and air photographs have shown that an equally large complex of farm buildings, enclosed by a wall and divided by a gravel road, still exists beneath adjoining farmland.

The most unified and magnificent plan was that of Woodchester (Gloucestershire) (figure 23), celebrated for its 'Great Pavement' (figure 24), which at 15 metres (48 feet 10 inches) square is the largest mosaic

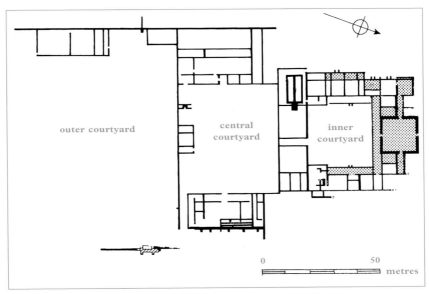

23. Woodchester (Gloucestershire): plan. (After S. Lysons and G. Clarke)

24. Woodchester: a portion of the 'Great Pavement', which was briefly revealed in 1963. One pillar of the colonnade is in the background. (Author)

25. This imaginary North African villa encapsulates many features that we are coming to recognise (albeit distantly) in our Romano-British villas. The bath-house is in the foreground. (From a mosaic in the Bardo Museum, Tunis)

yet discovered in Europe north of the Alps. As at North Leigh, this splendid mansion with its columned reception room and Orpheus mosaic was merely the nucleus of a more extensive establishment. With its sequence of courtyards, this palatial villa is more Mediterranean than British in character. It can be compared to villas in North Africa or Sicily. Figure 25 shows one of these in mosaic – an idealised North African landscape with towers and galleries in a park-like setting with exotic wildfowl.

4
Villas with a difference

The palace at Fishbourne (West Sussex) is in a class by itself – not only because of its exceptionally early date, but also because of its magnificence. Shortly after the conquest of AD 43 military buildings gave way first to a timber villa, then to its replacement in masonry (the 'Protopalace') and finally (between about AD 75 and 80) to what we see today, a palace fit for a king. The king in question was either the client king Cogodubnus or a senior official in the new provincial government. Visitors can still marvel at the mosaics, courtyards and formal gardens so skilfully recreated.

Nevertheless, looking at the excellent model in the museum (figure 26), one can easily forget two important points: first, that this was merely a nucleus of an estate that comprised private, park-like grounds sweeping southwards to the seashore and a small private harbour, around which, to the north, apparently spread a community of servants' quarters, workshops and farm buildings that have yet to be fully traced; second, that this 4 hectare (10 acre) building ceased to be a palace as early as

26. The palace at Fishbourne (West Sussex), as it may have looked in about AD 75. (Fishbourne Roman Palace/Sussex Archaeological Society)

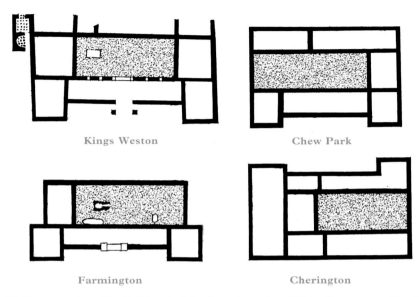

27. Four examples of the 'hall-type' of plan in south-western Britain. The owners evidently favoured the single, extended family house. This might reflect immigration from Gaul.

about AD 100 and was split up into separate units. Further modifications were abruptly terminated by a disastrous fire at the end of the third century, but the process if continued would have rendered Fishbourne virtually indistinguishable from any of the wealthier villas of Britain.

It is important to stress just how diverse these villas were. Purely local and regional variations can be detected in the ground plans of villa groups. For example, there is a small group (with outliers) in south-west Britain, each with a long central courtyard open to the air and usually gravelled (figure 27); the central feature is often a hearth, oven or water-tank, around which the other rooms were arranged. Clearly, this 'hall-type' plan implies an emphasis on the single, extended family. An attractive (if controversial) explanation suggests that this plan may reflect trouble in Gaul, especially between AD 260 and 276, when barbarian raids might have persuaded a group of Gaulish landowners to invest their capital in Britain and even settle there. In the third century much of the downlands had not yet been opened up to arable farming, and Cirencester and Bath would have offered the attractions of civilised life.

It is difficult to estimate how far villa owners collaborated with each other, and how far there was a pool of free (as distinct from slave) labour available at harvest and other times. We know that in other provinces, such as Africa, there were mobile teams of harvesters. Any proprietor had to calculate carefully how many workers he could afford to keep on the casual payroll, how many, by contrast, were resident staff and to what extent the remaining labour was to be provided from the tenant farms and native settlements. There is no evidence for slave labour in large gangs. On the other hand, anything that involved a higher degree of technology, such as a *vallus* or reaping machine, could have been shared within the estate.

We have already noted that agriculture was not the only basic activity of a villa; we can only guess at some of the others. Horse-breeding, for instance, is illustrated on the mosaics of North Africa but only surmised in Britain, yet the horse was essential for hunting, racing and sport, not to mention the cavalry. A more specialised activity – that of the private spa or 'health farm' – has been suggested for Gadebridge Park (Hertfordshire), with its great swimming-pool (figure 28). The 'industrial villas' could each have been the residence of the proprietor who acquired his wealth from a particular industry. The tile-works at Ashtead (Surrey), the salt-works at Droitwich (Worcestershire) and the pottery kilns at Castor/Water Newton (Cambridgeshire) and Orton Longueville (Cambridgeshire) all seem to owe their affluence and evident status to this source.

Another villa that seems, at first sight, to have an industrial connection is at Combe Down (Somerset), in the heart of the excellent stone quarries of Bath. But there is a difference; an inscription records the restoration

26. Gadebridge Park (Hertfordshire): a new model. The tower-like granaries used the warmth of the hypocausts below. Note the large swimming-pool – was this a health farm? (Dacorum Heritage Trust Ltd, Berkhamsted; model by George Rome Lanes)

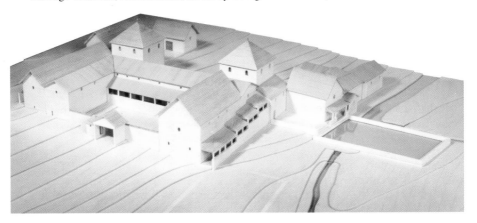

29. The tower at Stonea (Cambridgeshire), dominated the surrounding fenland as part of an imperial estate. (The British Museum)

of the *principia*, or headquarters. This military term could mean that the estate belonged to the emperor. The so-called 'imperial estates' are known and identifiable in many provinces; in Britain, however, they have proved disappointingly elusive. Since fine stone was often the prerogative of the emperor, the lead seals bearing the imperial title at the Combe Down villa may provide further clues to what we can call, generally, 'the state'.

Imperial estates were administered directly by the civil service and the army. Private estates, by contrast, were subject to taxation – both in cash (as in the case of death duties and income tax) and in kind (principally hides and corn). The techniques for collecting the *tributum* evolved considerably between the first and the fourth century AD. But one principle did not change: as far as possible Rome expected the provincials to collect the tribute themselves. The villa owner therefore had to produce an agreed surplus as tribute. He had to collect this surplus, store it and process it on the farm. Then it was checked by officials and sent on by road to one of the many *mansiones* or posting stations. Most of it would end up on the northern frontier of Britain, where the army's demand for leather and corn was prodigious. We sometimes try to identify the villas that acted as collection points. The large barns at Lullingstone (Kent) and Ditchley (Oxfordshire) might be such, the Stroud villa (Hampshire) another. At Hambleden (Buckinghamshire) there was a huge capacity for drying corn (figure 47) but no granaries for storing it, and the discovery of no fewer than seventy *stili* (bronze pens) on this villa points to a bureaucratic checking of the produce.

Tax collection was in effect the interface between the villa owner and officialdom. The republican system of collecting the tribute through the *publicani* was gradually modified and finally replaced, in about AD 200, by the *annona militaris*, or tax in kind. One area in which some scholars suspect the hand of the government and the imperial civil service is the Fens of East Anglia, from about AD 50. As the sea level fell and the wetlands became increasingly available for pasture and arable cultivation, so a new landscape evolved with canals, roads and

30. Gatcombe (Somerset): here a series of 'zones' is suggested, in which the villa was distinct from a range of workshops and other buildings, and the whole was enclosed by a unique defensive wall. (After K. Branigan)

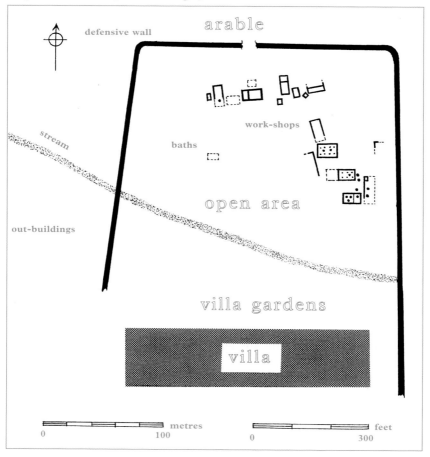

major engineering works designed to exploit the changes. A focus was the new establishment of Stonea (Cambridgeshire), a site that was part villa, part administrative centre and part small town. Created in about AD 120 – and an imaginative project that might have appealed to Hadrian – Stonea had at its heart a D-shaped complex with a piazza and a central tower that dominated the surrounding fens. Here markets would have been held and taxes paid. Sadly, this ambitious enterprise did not prosper, and within about fifty years the tower was demolished and the administrative system reorganised (figure 29).

Our last example, Gatcombe (Somerset), is sometimes considered to be not a villa at all but rather a settlement or even a small town (figure 30). There was undoubtedly a main house at one end of a garden area, and at least one mosaic is known. Workshops occupied the northern part – twenty-four of them in all. The trades of these workers, as provisionally identified, include milling and baking, a slaughterhouse with cold store, a forge and workshops for smelting and pewter. So Gatcombe combined villa and farm in one, seemingly arranged in four zones and with the most remarkable feature – a huge defensive wall in excellent masonry. The wall (and most of the buildings) is early to mid fourth century in date, so it is not to be compared with the fortified villas of the later fourth century in Germany. Nevertheless, the sheer extent of the walled circuit is remarkable in itself, and the ensemble is difficult to parallel anywhere in the world.

5
Architecture and interior decoration

From the earliest days of the occupation the standard of design and construction of British villas was as high as anywhere in the Empire. In particular, the bath suite displays a design as advanced as its way of life was alien to Britain. For the baths were more than a source of cleanliness: they were a warm, noisy and unhurried place of recreation and their decoration was often very lavish. At Chedworth (Gloucestershire), as in a few other villas, the bather was even offered a choice of two procedures – the 'Spartan' or the ordinary. The first entailed dry heat and high temperatures, on the sauna principle; the second, akin to the Turkish bath, used damp heat and plunge baths. The basic sequence is well exemplified in the small house (which can be visited) at Newport (Isle of Wight) (figure 31). From the unheated changing room (*apodyterium*) the bather passed through a warm room (*tepidarium*) – or two in this case – to the *caldarium*, which contained a hot bath. The hot, steamy atmosphere opened the pores of the skin and induced sweating; the dirt was removed not with soap but with oil and a curved *strigil*, or scraper. Massage could be part of the process, which continued with a leisurely return through the warm room to the *frigidarium*, to end with a sharp cold plunge and a rub down with a towel. In public baths the latrine is found here, flushed by the same water supply. Architecturally the baths could be the showpiece of the villa – at Lufton (Somerset), for instance (figure 32) – while the elaborate example at Stroud (Hampshire) (figure 42) was undoubtedly an amenity for a very large estate.

Complex bath suites were architecturally very sophisticated. The diagram in figure 31 illustrates the ingenuity with which the warmth was conserved and used. The hot air and gases passed under the hypocaust floor and up a jacket of box-flues concealed in the walls. Sometimes these vented under the eaves, but sometimes they led to hollow brick ribs. These distinctive voussoir-shaped flues have often gone unrecognised by excavators; they were used at Bignor (West Sussex), and a specimen has been placed in the museum. Tufa is a porous limestone similar to breeze-block, ideal for an insulated vault. The insulation was completed by narrow lancet windows, glazed with pale-green glass. The hot bath emptied into a drain, made of logs joined by iron collars. There were two kinds of hypocaust: the pillared variety could be heated more rapidly as required, while the masonry masses of the channelled kind acted like block-storage heaters and were more suitable for living-rooms.

Roofs were of thatch, tiles or stone slates, occasionally in combination,

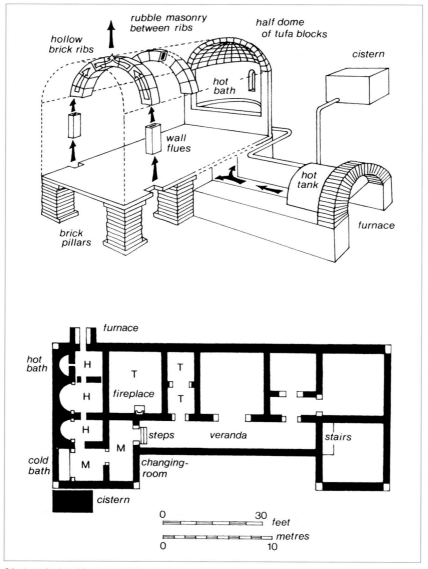

31. A typical *caldarium* with hot bath, showing details of plumbing and installation. (Below) The main house at Newport (Isle of Wight).

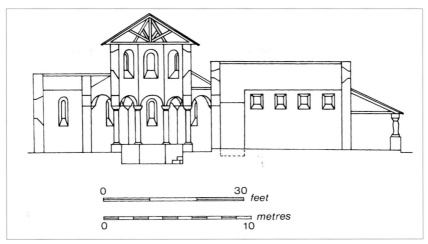

32. Lufton (Somerset): a conjectural elevation of the baths. (After C. B. Swaine)

crested with semicircular ridge-tiles and finished with terracotta or stone finials (figure 34). Most museums can demonstrate the characteristic combination of curved *imbrex* and flat *tegula* giving an effect similar to large pantiles.

Walls were generally timber-framed on low sill-walls, and the timbering was often rendered – though the scratched sketch of a villa from Hucclecote (Gloucestershire), now in the British Museum (figure 33), seems to show exposed timbers. Windows were sometimes glazed, despite the expense, the panes being held in place by cross-shaped iron devices where the window bars crossed. Wooden shutters must have been normal. Doors were either hinged or made with stout vertical pins

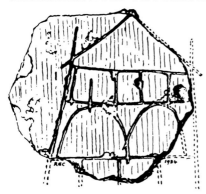

33. A villa sketched on the wall plaster at Hucclecote (Gloucestershire). (The British Museum, drawing by R. G. Collingwood)

34. Decorative stone roof finials from Dewlish (Dorset) (left), and Rockbourne (Hampshire) (right). (Bournemouth University and M. J. Locke)

turning in metal bushes in the lintel and threshold. Locks and keys can be found in most museums.

We have long been used to seeing bright colours used in the interiors of villas. Now the excavations at Piddington (Northamptonshire) have given us evidence of brightly coloured external walls. These were plastered and painted bright red; the short stubby columns were painted red, purple-brown and white. The *imbrex* tiles were deliberately fired to a garish sky-blue colour, while among other pigments used for the plaster was cinnabar (an expensive luxury from northern Spain). Bright

35. A typical Roman roof of limestone slates at Newport (Isle of Wight), using original slates. (David Tomalin)

36. The house at Piddington (Northamptonshire) with its colourful external décor. (R. Friendship-Taylor)

37. Newport (Isle of Wight): a reconstruction on the site of the colourful frescoes. The chequered black and white mosaic is original. So, too, is an unusual luxury – a fireplace.

colours were perfect for the interior décor, and good modern excavation is constantly recovering excellent, if fragmentary, murals. Wall mosaics were rare, but most villas could boast one or more fine mosaic floors, and wherever possible these are now displayed on the site. Cheaper floors were of coarse red *tesserae*, perhaps with carpets, or of concrete, pink plaster or even bare earth. A few houses had painted ceilings.

Of furniture we know disappointingly little; the elegant rooms recreated in the museums of Cirencester and London show what could have been found in any well-appointed villa, with cupboards, sideboards and occasional tables set against the walls. The classical dining-room, the *triclinium* (or, more commonly in the later period, the semicircular *stibadium*), can be recognised, in which the diners reclined on couches arranged in threes. Often – but by no means always – the dining-room had a prominent apse (at Lullingstone in Kent, for instance), while we must remember that Roman taste distinguished summer and winter dining-rooms. This, however, is high-status dining; normally in the north-western provinces people ate at tables with chairs or couches in square dining-rooms.

Finally, the existence of upper floors is much debated. Walls of exceptional thickness and narrow rooms that might have contained stairs are thought to be clues. At Chalk (Kent) the wooden stairs survived, with cupboard space below, and at Thurnham (Kent) it now seems certain that there was an upper floor. Indeed, it is now generally believed that the more ambitious villas followed Roman practice elsewhere and had at least two storeys.

38. Thurnham (Kent): the excavations for the Channel Tunnel Rail Link in 2000, seen from the north, showing the main house. One of the pre-Roman houses can be made out in the foreground. (Oxford Archaeology. Copyright CTRL [UK] Limited)

6
Aisled barns and other buildings

The Thurnham plan reminds us that a villa was seldom a single building, built at a single time. Our simplified plan shows how an early Roman 'proto-villa' (in red) was replaced by a two-storey house. Inside and outside the ditched enclosure are represented all the varied activities of the farm. These include a well, a corn-drier and a possible temple.

Second in importance only to the house is the prominent aisled building. Many villas had one of these; a few had two. They were probably used for storing equipment and produce (but never, it seems, animals). Certainly they housed large numbers of people and gave cover for indoor activities such as corn-drying and metalworking. At Sparsholt (Hampshire) a single cooking range against one wall was surrounded by ashes and trampled food debris – clearly a communal kitchen and focal point on cold winter evenings.

The conjectural reconstruction of a typical example in figure 40 shows a cart-sized entrance at one side (or sometimes at the end), a construction on low sleeper-walls and stone pillar-bases, and a simple roof carried

39. Thurnham (Kent): simplified plan showing the unbroken sequence from the later Iron Age to the early fourth century AD. (Copyright CTRL [UK] Limited)

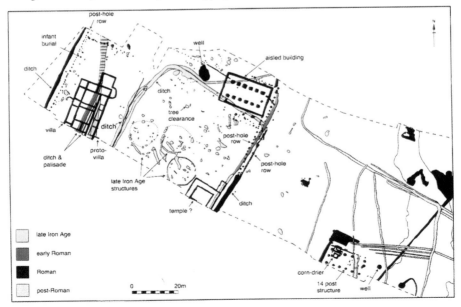

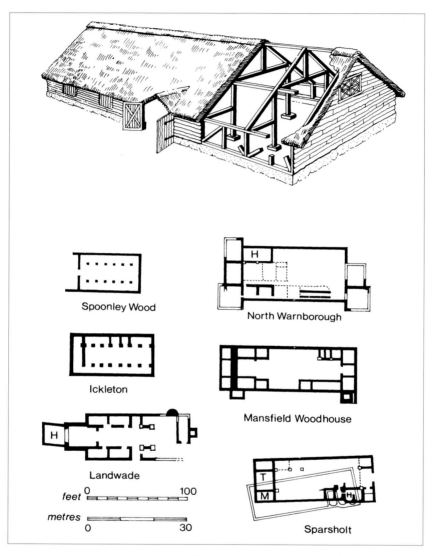

40. A typical aisled building and some excavated examples.

41. At Meonstoke (Hampshire), the collapsed façade of the aisled building (shown in this reconstruction) indicates the steep roof-pitch. Although the building was used mainly for agricultural storage, the colourful and elaborate architecture is noteworthy. (The British Museum)

down to the walls in a single sweep, with a hayloft above. Opinions vary, however, on the single sweep, and Meonstoke (Hampshire) provides an alternative solution to the problem of lighting and ventilation. Meonstoke may be exceptionally grand and ornate for an aisled barn, and its roof-pitch surprisingly steep, but the elevation is authentic, as the collapsed remains were found virtually entire. Aisled buildings are very common in Britain; the type is best regarded as a British invention, though closely similar buildings occasionally occur on the Continent.

Privacy was at a premium and many aisled buildings show signs of temporary partitions making improvised compartments or rooms. These would 'fossilise' and become more permanent, so that in some evolved examples only the proportions and a few surviving pillar-bases reveal the original layout. Occasionally, as at Brading (Isle of Wight), baths for the whole community were incorporated. Often, as at North Warnborough (Hampshire), this was the farmhouse; in time it underwent extensive modifications including a kind of modernisation with twin towers, or wings, added to improve the façade. Sparsholt is unique in having two aisled buildings, apparently of similar plan, one replacing the other. Here the owner eventually moved out and constructed his

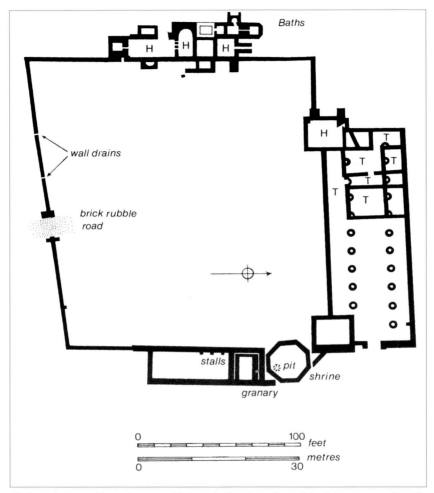

42. Stroud (Hampshire): the unusually large bath suite and possible shrine suggest that this was the focus of a large estate. The stalls were probably for three plough-teams of oxen, and the wall drains imply either an unrecognised timber lean-to or a dung-heap.

new bungalow nearby (figure 54); before he moved, however, he had created three private rooms for himself and his family in the aisled house, one with a tessellated floor, another with a mosaic. Perhaps he left these to his farm manager. A pair of heavily modified aisled buildings can be detected on the plan of Brading (figure 52).

The barn or granary was another necessary building, sometimes detached (as in the corner of the Ditchley villa in Oxfordshire, to the right of the entrance), but often incorporated in the range of outbuildings. The raised floor is sometimes indicated by an offset in the walls (for example at Stroud, Hampshire, figure 42) or by parallel supporting walls (such as at North Warnborough), and frequently by buttresses (the north-eastern block at Woodchester, Gloucestershire, for instance). The dimensions sometimes enable a reasoned guess to be made at other buildings; three stalls, for example, in the long barn at Stroud could have held three teams of oxen, while twelve plough-teams could have been accommodated in a long building in the yard at Bignor (West Sussex). An earlier long building (later demolished) at Bignor is interpreted as a cattle-shed, and the small granary at Stroud suggests the grain-fattening of pigs in the adjoining building.

A regular feature of any villa was the well. The importance of water cannot be overestimated, and wells were often of immense depths. Naturally, water was needed not merely for drinking and having hot baths but also, importantly, for the overwintering of cattle. This was now more feasible because of the new water supply – plus, of course, the provision of cowsheds and plenty of fodder.

A rare find at Stanwick (Northamptonshire) may have been evidence for a donkey mill. The stones of the circular track are worn as though by the ceaseless tread of animals. Two watermills are known from British villas. At one, Fullerton (Hampshire), the miller's house had good mosaics but lacked the usual agricultural outbuildings. The mill-race, the leats and one millstone survived and the mill presumably provided this specialised service over a wide area. At Fullerton both mill and villa date from the fourth century. The other watermill, at Redlands Farm (Northamptonshire), was of the first century. Here, too, branching leats could be traced, but the actual house was very basic – a two-roomed structure that probably included the mill itself. This mill had a short life and was replaced by a classic winged-corridor villa.

Finally, an isolated outbuilding of a lost villa at Chalk (Kent), excavated by the author, excited some speculation. It was an oblong one-roomed house with timber-framed walls, painted wall plaster and a tiled roof. Positioned near the entrance to the complex, it might have belonged to the bailiff. Below it was a cellar, entered by wooden steps, lit by lamps in niches and with a ramp for rolling down barrels. It was a wine cellar, of a pattern commonly found in Kent. Later this received painted wall plaster and became a dwelling. In its final phase, however, this basement is thought to have been an *ergastulum*, or slave prison. Large fetters were found, and infant burials in the floor. One of its last occupants had sat near the doorway making pins from antler and jet. Here we found

43. At Piddington (Northamptonshire) there was good evidence for this elaborate well-head. (R. Friendship-Taylor)

his pewter dish and spoon, his knife and a whetstone. A discarded boot (or at least its studs) completed the untidy picture.

Whether this villa employed slaves elsewhere we shall never know for certain, but one pottery sherd strengthens the suggestion (figure 44), as it was inscribed in Greek characters *FELICI* (*TER*) – 'To Felix', or perhaps 'Good luck'. A Greek clerk would certainly have been an asset on any Romano-British villa.

44. A pottery sherd inscribed with Greek letters, from Chalk, Gravesend (Kent). (University of Southampton)

7
The villa estate

The Frocester Court villa (Gloucestershire) (figure 45) illustrates the diversity of a typical estate, focused on the 'office' with its strongbox, central hearth and coin scatter. The living-rooms were in the south-east corner (probably on two floors), with the 'corn room' (corn-drier and quern) later converted into a kitchen. About AD 360 the baths were added in place of the open-fronted 'wool shed' in which quantities of fuller's earth were found, for fulling and felting. Close to the villa was a dipping pool, and a sheep-bell was among the finds. The western paddock could have been useful for animals awaiting shoeing at the forge or milking. Horse bones, especially those of young animals, were comparatively common and oats were certainly grown, so commercial horse-breeding is a possibility. Pannage for pigs would have been provided by forests on the estate, and bones of chicken, duck and goose have also been found.

An equally varied landscape can be deduced, in more detail, at Bignor (West Sussex) (figure 46). The estate, running to perhaps 1000 hectares (2500 acres) in all, may have had cereals and other crops on about 300

45. Frocester Court (Gloucestershire), in the early fourth century AD, with suggested use of rooms. Residential quarters on the ground floor are shaded and stairs are asterisked.

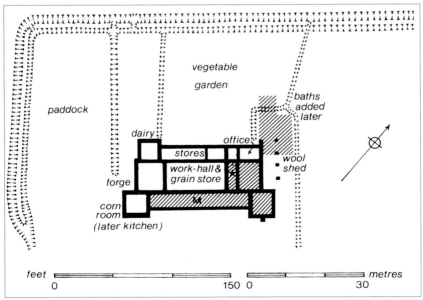

hectares (750 acres) of good arable land, fifty or more cattle out to pasture in the valley-bottom meadows, two hundred sheep up on the downland and an unknown number of pigs in the woods. A workforce at Bignor of between thirty and fifty hands is estimated.

The crops at Frocester Court – barley, three varieties of wheat and oats – were described by a specialist as 'well-grown, clean, healthy crops which had been harvested and stored under ideal conditions'.

46. Bignor (West Sussex): an analysis of the villa estate – varied landscape supporting a regime of mixed farming. (After S. Applebaum and N. Faulkner)

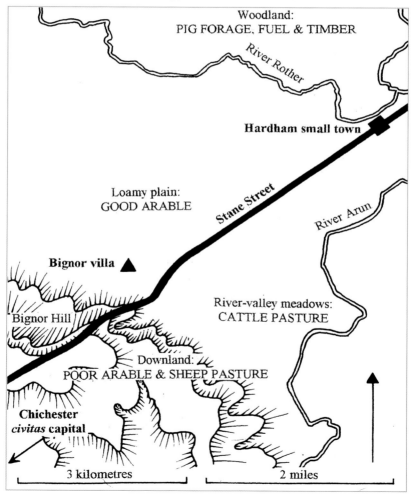

Woodland:
PIG FORAGE, FUEL & TIMBER

River Rother

Hardham small town

Loamy plain:
GOOD ARABLE

Stane Street

River Arun

Bignor villa ▲

River-valley meadows:
CATTLE PASTURE

Bignor Hill

Downland:
POOR ARABLE & SHEEP PASTURE

Chichester
civitas capital

3 kilometres

2 miles

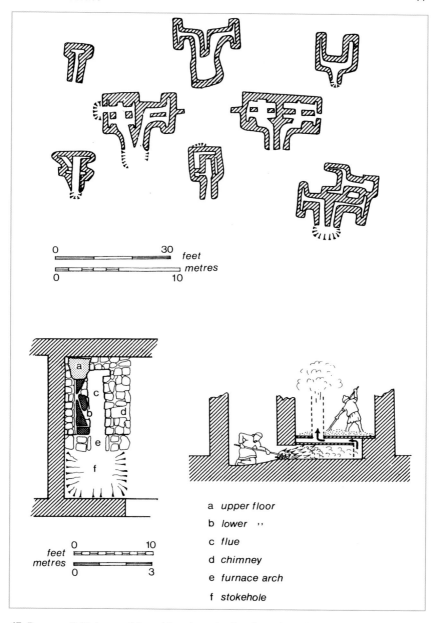

a *upper floor*

b *lower* ,,

c *flue*

d *chimney*

e *furnace arch*

f *stokehole*

47. Romano-British corn-driers: (above) a selection from the series at the Hambleden villa (Buckinghamshire); (below) Atworth (Wiltshire).

Other Romano-British farmers – to judge from analysed samples – were more tolerant of weeds, even perhaps encouraging a deliberate mixture. Cereals were not only for human consumption but also for grain-fattening of pigs for bacon; other crops such as rape, vetch and turnip, as well as hay, were winter feed for cattle. Straw was more readily available as the new low-cutting scythe had superseded the prehistoric practice of cutting only the ears.

Crop rotation was recommended by Roman textbooks, as was the sowing of both spring and winter wheat, and the importance of manure can be deduced from the use of animal pens and the distribution of household debris in fields far from the house. Viticulture, although officially permitted, was not widespread. An important development, which matches the pre-Roman change from storing grain in pits to granaries, is the construction of 'corn-driers' (figure 47); parching facilitates threshing and milling and prevents germination in store. However, modern experiments have suggested that they are inefficient at drying corn, although they are ideal for malting.

A particularly elaborate implement was the *vallus*, or reaping machine. Powered by an ox and guided by one (or sometimes two) assistants, it had sharpened wooden blades. The forward motion cut the ears and

48. A replica *vallus*, or harvesting machine, that was used at the Butser Ancient Farm in Hampshire. (Peter Reynolds)

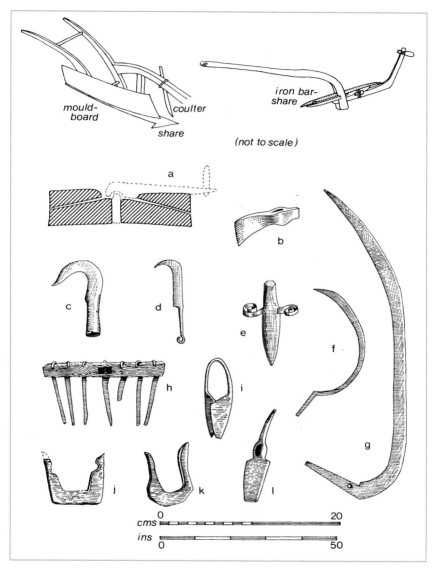

49. (Above) A plough of the Roman type and a typical Iron Age ard. (Below) Farm implements from British sites: *(a)* oscillatory quern; *(b)* axe; *(c)* billhook; *(d)* pruning hook; *(e)* mower's anvil; *(f)* sickle; *(g)* scythe; *(h)* wooden hay-rake; *(i)* sheep shears; *(j, k)* iron bindings for wooden spades; *(l)* mattock or hoe.

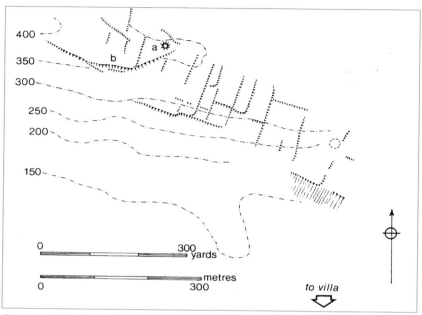

50. Fields associated with the Brading villa. At *a* a Bronze Age barrow has been incorporated and at *b* there are traces of a flattened pre-Roman earthwork, perhaps a hillfort. Contours are in feet.

dropped them into a collecting box. The straw was then scythed for thatching, burnt or ploughed in.

A range of tools is illustrated in figure 49, and most are known as types familiar to us today. The quern is a hand-mill (properly known as an 'oscillatory' rather than a 'rotary' quern as the movement was roughly a quarter-turn). This was a pre-Roman invention for domestic use, while the large villa could afford a full-size animal-driven mill. Spades were of wood, edged with iron, and spade cultivation in ridged 'lazy-beds' is a technique recognised near Godmanchester (Cambridgeshire) and in the Fens. Spades, too, account for the distinctive V-shape of Roman drainage ditches. Villa fields have been distinguished from 'Celtic' fields of traditional native type. In figures 50 and 51 two well-known and contrasting cases are shown. At Barnsley Park (Gloucestershire) it is not clear which are paddocks, hoe-plots and ploughed fields. On Brading Down (Isle of Wight), however, the oblong shape is attributed to the use of a heavier plough (figure 49, top left), pulled in one direction and requiring fewer turns at the headland. The coulter cuts the turf and the mouldboard turns a furrow, whose depth is regulated by the share.

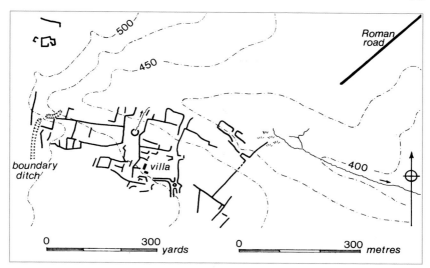

51. Emparkment at Barnsley Park (Gloucestershire), has preserved the faint earthworks of Roman fields and enclosures. Those immediately to the north, west and south of the villa are stone-walled, and were perhaps stockyards. Selective excavation has suggested a complex history extending into the fifth century AD. Contours are in feet.

The more primitive ard (on the right) merely grooved the soil but continued to be used through the period on the terraced lynchets and more rectangular plots that still miraculously survive on the southern downs. Such plots were cross-ploughed and often prepared by hoeing.

Although we now know a good deal about some individual estates, and regional studies are being energetically pursued, we are not yet able to paint a general picture of the economics of the villa system in Britain. We must accept some major uncertainties, such as the size of the labour force and the relationship between villas and native settlements, where much of the labour force lived. Total acreages of estates are much disputed, and the effect of a steadily deteriorating climate has yet to be identified. The balance between resident and absentee landlords, the independence or grouping of villas and the interplay of urban magistracies and landowning gentry in the *civitas* or local government region are all matters that cannot readily be settled from archaeological evidence alone. The orthodox view that villas were clustered around towns and related to major roads is not borne out either by the known distribution or by the little we understand of overland routes and rural markets. Scholarly interest has shifted away from the bricks-and-mortar aspects to the social and economic significance of the villas. In this respect particularly the study of Roman Britain has far to go.

8
The end of the villas

In order to understand what happened to the villas of later Roman Britain we must glance briefly at developments in the rest of Europe. During the troubled years of the fourth century AD all the provinces of the western empire suffered acute manpower shortages. This had to be made good somehow. Italy itself was under attack, and by AD 467 the western provinces had effectively lost control of their territory to outsiders. These barbarians were not so much armed invaders as immigrant settlers. Their dominance took many forms, political and cultural, ranging from peaceful assimilation to the less comfortable presence of Germanic troops officially employed as garrisons in both town and country. The towns still offered some security; in some areas, however, villa owners were frightened of armed bandits and feared for their livestock and crops. A poignant reminder of insecurity in the countryside is the corn-drier at Brading (Isle of Wight) that was dug through the mosaic of the main house, perhaps in a moment of panic. Nevertheless, in comparison with its European counterparts Britain in

52. Brading (Isle of Wight), as excavated. In its latest phase the main house has been gutted and partly re-roofed, forming an open-fronted work-hall and stores. A corn-drier has been inserted through the tessellated floor.

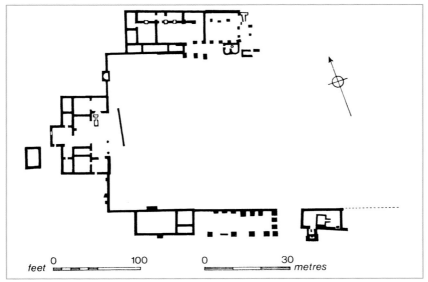

feet 0   100   0   30 metres

the fourth century actually seemed relatively stable (even attracting investment in land from overseas investors).

We still have to account for the eventual disappearance of the British villas. It would be wrong to think of this as a single event. First the withdrawal of the legions, then the loss of financial support and ultimately of administrative services – these are well documented. What is less clear is the stages, between about AD 350 and 500, of the gradual transformation in Britain from a Roman to what would become a medieval landscape.

In the 1950s many believed that in most of Britain the Anglo-Saxon invaders of the fifth and sixth centuries found a largely depopulated landscape. This may not be so: a more recent study (*c*.1995) suggests that in much of Britain the population may have remained steady. True, there were population shifts, such as the mass migrations to Brittany in 470, offset from time to time by the acquisition of new territory by immigrant settlers. However, many villas were undoubtedly abandoned, and on the whole we do not know why this happened – or even when. For after about AD 400 we are bereft of our aids to close dating (principally coins and pottery) in a kind of chronological no man's land. Even when we can suggest a date it is usually impossible to relate the end of a villa to any known event.

Perhaps the 'abandonment' model disguises a fundamental change of attitude. All too often we dismiss excavated features as 'squatter occupation' – mosaics patched with stone slabs or cut through by a corn-drier (such as at Brading), or bricks from a disused bath-house used for a new oven (at Sparsholt, Hampshire, for example). But here we may be seeing not squalor but a cultural shift; in other words there was no longer any need for mosaics and luxurious baths in a new world in which the fields continued to be ploughed and the cows milked as before but now free from the tax-gatherer and the absentee landlord.

This is no fantasy, as on many villas we are able to identify a sub-Roman phase within the Roman period – the final phases, for example, of the two villas in figures 53 and 54 are both dated to the middle of the fourth century. At Sparsholt the fields continued to be cultivated and the walled yard was maintained as a stockyard, with partial occupation of the derelict aisled building and the creation of a new timbered hall outside the ruins. At Gadebridge Park (Hertfordshire) the baths and villa were demolished and stockades or cattle pens were built over the earlier buildings. Only one small cottage (figure 57) remained in occupation. At Latimer (Buckinghamshire) the abandonment of the villa was a gradual, orderly process in the later fourth century; it may be one of the villas that we believe were granted to the Germanic mercenary soldiers (in this case the garrison of neighbouring St Albans), for the

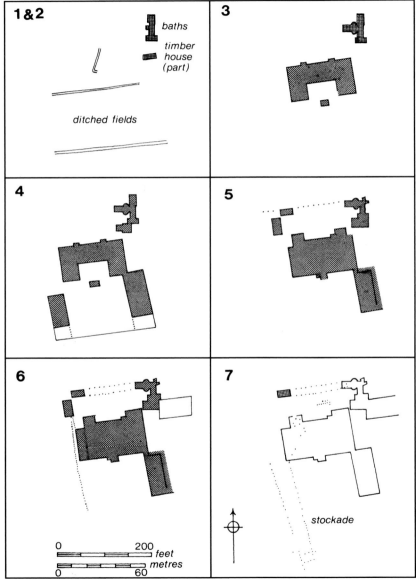

53. The evolution of the Gadebridge Park villa (Hertfordshire), from the late first to the fourth century AD. In the final phase the baths and villa were demolished and stockades or cattle pens were built on their sites.

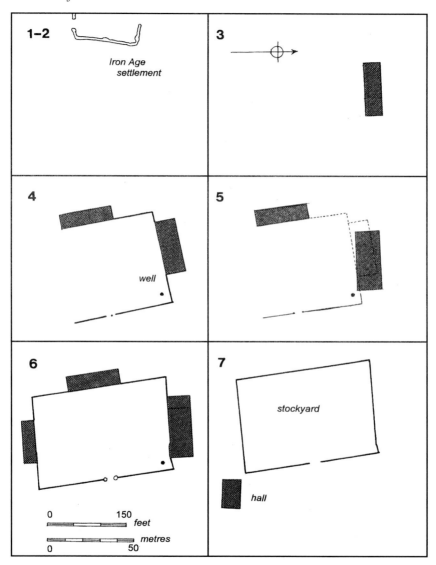

54. Sparsholt (Hampshire): the evolution of the villa. The pre-Roman site was reoccupied in *c*.AD 250 until perhaps 450, when the ruins were replaced by a timbered 'hall'.

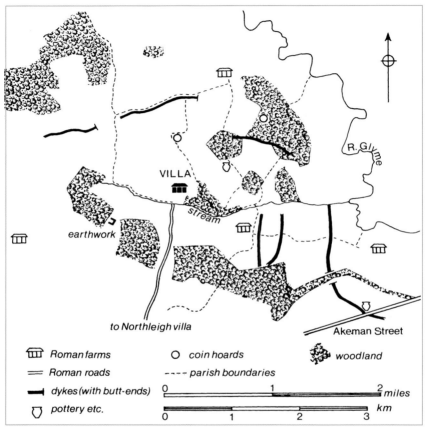

55. Continuity in the landscape at Ditchley Park (Oxfordshire). The main villa is shown in figure 19.

succeeding cruck-built hall (figure 56) and adjoining barn are best paralleled in Westphalia. There were four successive sub-Roman buildings and phases lasting well into the Dark Ages of the fifth century, perhaps beyond. These three sites can now be matched by many others; in each the story is slightly different, but they all have this in common: the new way of life and standards of building leave little archaeological trace.

The most likely suggestion, therefore, is that the estates continued to be cultivated as before but free from the pressures of central government, while the domestic buildings were abandoned. What happened next is illustrated at Rockbourne (Hampshire). The skeleton in the north-west

56. The fourth-century post-villa building at Latimer (Buckinghamshire), as excavated. Its cruck-built construction is shown by the settings for upright timbers just inside the walls. (K. Branigan)

corner was evidently someone killed by falling masonry in the collapsed and derelict building. An artist's impression (figure 58) shows these scavengers at work. Alternatively, the ruins were effectively marginal land and likely to remain undisturbed, so we find that empty villas were

57. The two-roomed cottage of the fifth century at Gadebridge Park (Hertfordshire), as excavated. The kitchen, with ovens, hearth and storage cist, is the further room. (J. Brown)

used for cemeteries and isolated burials; Rockbourne is one such site.

It appears that habitations were either dispersed or nucleated around the old sites, forming the beginnings of new villages. The continental evidence for this is strong (though a notable lack in Britain is of the fortified, château-like villas). An adaptation of this pattern to Britain would be to suggest the gradual transformation of the villa estate into the medieval manor, especially if, as some believe, feudalism was foreshadowed in the later Empire. So medieval evidence, Saxon estates and parish boundaries are now being examined in the hope of tracing the process backwards in time. One area in which the villa estate has been traced in modern landscape is around the Ditchley villa (figure 55) in Oxfordshire, now largely the estate of its successor, Ditchley Park. Excavation has shown the boundary dykes to be Roman, the gaps between the butt-ends presumably being filled by woodland. Archaeological and documentary evidence suggests that much of the present woodland is ancient, so we can visualise an almost complete circuit of earthwork and forest with a radius of about 1.2 km (^{3}/4 mile) around the villa at its centre. The enclosed area of about 354 hectares (875 acres) is bisected by a stream at the bottom of a steep valley and by the approach road to the villa. Within this area can still be seen traces of ancient fields, and at least one subsidiary farm seems to be within the part enclosed by the dykes. The villa itself had a substantial granary, so the other sites shown in figure 55 may well have been tenant farms outside the estate proper. The country house that succeeded it is less than a mile to the north-west, and the fact that parish boundaries follow much of the presumed Roman boundary suggests that there was here some unit already recognisable in Saxon times.

58. Post-Roman scavengers in the derelict Rockbourne villa. The painting (based on the excavations) shows the scene before the man in the foreground was killed by the falling masonry. (Michael Codd and Hampshire County Council)

9
Further reading

General works

The best introduction to Roman villas might be found in a general work on Roman Britain, such as *Roman Britain* by M. Millett (Batsford/English Heritage, 1995) or, more substantially, *Roman Britain* by T. W. Potter and C. Johns (British Museum Press, 1992); for more background try J. Alcock's *Life in Roman Britain* (Batsford/English Heritage, 1996). A readable account of the fourth-century floruit is G. de la Bédoyère's *The Golden Age of Roman Britain* (Tempus, 1999), which contrasts with a more sombre and individual interpretation by N. Faulkner in *The Decline and Fall of Roman Britain* (Tempus, 2000). Orthodoxy here (as far as it is ever possible) is provided by Stephen Johnson in *Later Roman Britain* (Routledge & Kegan Paul, 1980).

For a more cerebral and challenging essay try M. Millett's *The Romanization of Britain* (Cambridge, 1990), and a useful synthesis of the environmental aspects is to be found in *The Landscape of Roman Britain* by K. and P. Dark (Alan Sutton, 1997). Some stimulating ideas appear in G. de la Bédoyère's *Roman Villas and the Countryside* (Batsford/English Heritage, 1992).

For villas in general the standard work in English is J. Percival's *The Roman Villa: An Historical Introduction* (Batsford, 1976), which has the outstanding merit of treating villas as part of the social and economic life of the Roman world. This Empire-wide view can be supplemented by, for instance, A. G. McKay's *Houses, Villas and Palaces in the Roman World* (Thames & Hudson, 1975) and K. D. White's *Roman Farming* (Thames & Hudson, 1970).

For Britain, two valuable works are anthologies of varying aspects by several authors. The earlier is *The Roman Villa in Britain*, edited by A. L. F. Rivet (Routledge & Kegan Paul, 1969), complemented by *Studies in the Romano-British Villa*, edited by M. Todd (Leicester University Press, 1978).

Aspects of villa studies

The place of villas in the overall picture of rural life was established in *Rural Settlement in Roman Britain*, edited by A. C. Thomas (CBA Research Report number 7, London, 1966) and discussed in copious, if not always accurate, detail by S. Applebaum in *The Agrarian History of England* 1 (ii), edited by H. P. R. Finberg (Cambridge University Press, 1972); see also P. Morris's *Agricultural Buildings in Roman Britain* (British Archaeological Report number 70, Oxford, 1979).

For the relationship with the towns, the standard work is A. L. F. Rivet's *Town and Country in Roman Britain* (Hutchinson, 1958); a slighter and more localised essay on the same theme is K. Branigan's *Town and Country: Verulamium and the Roman Chilterns* (Spurbooks, 1973). A pioneer publication was *The Economies of Romano-British Villas*, edited by K. Branigan and D. Miles (University of Sheffield, 1987).

Regional studies

Two important regional surveys are K. Branigan's *The Roman Villa in South-west England* (Moonraker Press, 1977) and E. W. Black's *The Roman Villas of South-east England* (British Archaeological Report number 171, Oxford, 1987). There is also much of importance in *The Roman West Country* by K. Branigan and P. J. Fowler (David & Charles, Newton Abbot, 1976).

59. Villas that can be visited. Of the many archaeological guides and gazetteers the fullest is R. J. A. Wilson's *A Guide to the Roman Remains in Britain* (fourth edition, 2002). See also *Discovering Roman Britain* by D. E. Johnston (Shire Publications, third edition, 2002).

10
Villas to visit

Few of the villas listed below are visible in anything like their entirety, and there is only one in the north of England that can be visited (Beadlam). Grid references (used by permission of the Controller of Her Majesty's Stationery Office), instructions for finding each site and (where possible) a telephone number are given. Other details, however, are liable to change without notice, and visitors are advised to check before making a special journey. More detail will be found in the third edition of *Discovering Roman Britain* (Shire Publications, 2002).

Bancroft, Milton Keynes (SP 827403). *The villa lies north-west of Milton Keynes in Mills Way, Bradwell. Approach via the A422 (H3) from the A5 and turn left at the second roundabout. The site is part of the city parks network; there is a car park and access is not restricted. No telephone.*

Originally a straightforward winged-corridor house, this villa eventually acquired a walled garden, a central fish-pond, an octagonal summer-house and a mausoleum. The principal rooms have been marked out and the fish-pond reconstructed. The mosaics have been lifted, and one is prominently displayed in the Queen's Court shopping centre, Milton Keynes.

Beadlam, NorthYorkshire (SE 634842). *The villa is immediately north of the junction of the A170 Pickering–Helmsley road and a minor road to Harome. It is*

60. Winter in the villa at Brading (Isle of Wight). The main house is in the background of this courtyard villa. (Michael Codd and Oglander Roman Trust)

61. Brading (Isle of Wight): the new cover building. (Jan Toms)

an open site maintained by English Heritage. No telephone.

The only visitable villa north of the Humber, this well-preserved site was excavated in 1966–9. Of the three wings the best-preserved has been consolidated. It had a hypocaust with a damaged mosaic (in store). The other wing had a small bath-house.

Bignor, Pulborough, West Sussex RH20 1PH (SU 988147). *The villa lies east of the village of Bignor on a minor road from Bury to Bignor, 8 km (5 miles) south-west of Pulborough. Open regularly in summer. Telephone: 01798 869259.*

The main residential quarters are attractively set out, with earlier phases indicated in coloured concrete. Mosaics are displayed *in situ* within a group of buildings that resemble a straggling Roman villa. There is a site museum.

Brading, Morton Old Road, Brading, Isle of Wight PO36 0EN (SZ 599853). *The villa lies 800 metres (¹/₂ mile) south of Brading, off the A3055. Open daily. Telephone: 01983 406223. Website: www.bradingromanvilla.org.uk*

This fine villa, excavated in 1880, has been furnished with a new cover building and presentation, with a new museum. Most of the courtyard and the main block can be visited and the mystical mosaics are noteworthy.

Chedworth, Yanworth, near Cheltenham, Gloucestershire GL54 3LJ (SP 053134). *This National Trust property is off the A429 at Fossebridge, signposted along the road from Yanworth to Withington. Open regularly. Telephone: 01242 890256. Website: www.nationaltrust.org.uk*

The complete villa is displayed in an attractive rural setting, with the main house

62. This model of the Bignor villa in West Sussex looks out through the veranda, with its vivid colouring. (Worthing Museum)

63. Chedworth (Gloucestershire): a well-maintained villa in an attractive setting. The gallery in the foreground protects the mosaics.

(with mosaics) and baths undercover. There is a fine visitors' centre and a museum; the old-fashioned cover building of the west wing is due for modernisation.

Combley, Isle of Wight (SZ 537878). *The villa lies within the Robin Hill Adventure Park, Downend Road, 3 km (2 miles) east of Newport. From the A3054 turn right along Long Lane. The Robin Hill entrance is beside a mini-roundabout. The villa is open (free) when the park is open.*

Excavated in 1968–79, the house has been marked out in modern materials with explanatory signs. As at Great Witcombe, the sloping and unstable site caused problems from the start and probably caused its apparently premature end shortly after AD 375.

Fishbourne, Salthill Road, Fishbourne, Chichester, West Sussex PO19 3QS (SU 838047). *2.4 km (1¹/₂ miles) west of Chichester, turn north off the A27 into Salthill Road (signposted 'Roman Palace'). The site belongs to the Sussex Archaeological Society and is regularly open. Telephone: 01243 785859. Website: www.sussexpast.co.uk*

Whether this palace was a gift from the emperor or the residence of a high-ranking official, Fishbourne is unique for its exceptionally early date and for its magnificence. Its full extent, including its outbuildings, is unknown; of the palace proper one half is bisected by a main road and houses but the other half is under an elegant cover building. There are fine mosaics (including some from elsewhere in the area) and the reconstructed garden of the palace is noteworthy. The small harbour cannot be visited.

Fordcroft, St Mary Cray, Kent (TQ 467676). *The site lies between Poverest Road and Bellfield Road, close to the junction with the A224 Cray Avenue. The site is administered by Bromley Museum and can be visited by arrangement. Telephone: 01689 873826.*

Of this partly excavated villa three rooms of the detached bath-house have been conserved under a modern cover building. The villa was occupied through the fourth century until at least AD 550, when it was used as an Anglo-Saxon cemetery.

Great Witcombe, Gloucestershire (SO 899142). *The villa is signposted on the A417, 400 metres (440 yards) east of the crossroads with the A46. It is then 2.4 km (1¹/₂ miles) south of the road along a rough track past Droy's Court. The car park is a little distance beyond. This is an open site, managed by English Heritage; the bath-house mosaics are locked but the key is available from Corinium Museum, Cirencester. Telephone: 01285 655611.*

As at Combley, the beautiful site of this villa proved treacherous as the hillside is riddled with springs and soil slip necessitated constant buttressing and rebuilding. Two rooms have been independently identified as shrines to the water spirits of the site. One is the prominent octagonal room in the middle (which replaced an earlier room); the other is in the centre of the west wing, containing three niches and a central basin set in the floor.

Keynsham, Somerset (ST 645692). *The A4175 runs on an embankment across the villa site, most of which lay in the town cemetery.*

This fine villa was effectively destroyed in 1922–4 and now all that can be seen are some steps in the cemetery between the mortuary chapel and the road. A small separate Roman building (doubtless one of the outbuildings) was rebuilt near the entrance to the nearby factory. The Roman building, in its turn, is in 2004 under threat from redevelopment. The mosaics (formerly on view in the factory museum) are safely stored but inaccessible, and (to end this sorry tale) even their long-term future is now under review.

Kings Weston, Long Cross, Lawrence Weston, Bristol BS11 0LP (ST 534776). *South-west of Bristol via the A4 or M5 (junction 18). To visit, go to Blaise Castle House Museum, Henbury (telephone: 0117 903 9818) or Bristol City Museum (telephone: 0117 922 3571) for instructions on how to find the site. Website: www.bristol-city.gov.uk*

There were two buildings here, at right-angles. The eastern was of the 'hall' type with an internal yard (see figure 27) and a small porch. The other, now protected by a cover building, comprised a small bath suite and two large reception rooms with mosaics. One mosaic was damaged beyond recovery and has been replaced with another found not far away at Brislington.

Littlecote Park, Littlecote House Hotel, Littlecote, Hungerford, Berkshire RG17 0SS (SU 300704). *Approach from the B4192 and the byroad between Chilton Foliat and Froxfield and proceed along the drive past Littlecote House, west of which is the villa. The house is now a hotel; visitors are welcome to examine the villa in the grounds at all reasonable times. Telephone: 01488 682509.*

Known since 1730 and virtually rediscovered in 1978 and onwards, the entire extent of this elaborate villa with outbuildings can be explored in the park. The river Kennet provided an attractive setting for a detached summer dining-room

64. Lullingstone (Kent): two (of three) water-nymphs painted in a niche in the 'Deep Room' and later damaged when the basement became a Christian house-church. Fortunately this water-colour was made at the time of discovery: very little can now be discerned. (A. T. Rook)

(or perhaps a shrine) with a spectacular mosaic (under a cover).

Lullingstone, Lullingstone Lane, Eynsford, Dartford, Kent DA4 0JA (TQ 529651). *The villa lies north-west of Eynsford on a side road off the A225. The site is in the care of English Heritage. Telephone: 01322 863467.*
Most of this handsome villa, with fine mosaics, cult rooms and a good bath suite, is under a modern building with a riverside setting. Note the early Christian frescoes (in the British Museum but replicated here). Outside and uphill a small temple has been marked out, but the temple-mausoleum and the large barn are not visible.

Newport, Cypress Road, Newport, Isle of Wight PO30 1HE (SZ 501885). *The villa is in Cypress Road, which is off the A3056. It is in the care of the Isle of Wight Council and is open regularly. Telephone: 01983 529720 (summer) and 529963 (winter). Website: www.iow.gov.uk*
This winged-corridor villa of fourteen rooms including a bath suite is preserved under a modern cover building. There is an exhibition room and a display that deals with the entire island. Outside are an attractive Roman garden and a stone-built Roman corn-drier recovered from a field in Newchurch.

North Leigh, Oxfordshire (SP 397154). *The villa is signposted off the A4095. It is at East End, not North Leigh. There is a short walk from the car park. The site is in the care of English Heritage and is open daily. Telephone: 01483 304869 (for information on when the cover building is open).*
Conservation has laid out the final form of this courtyard villa with rooms on

65. Newport (Isle of Wight): a quiet corner of the reconstructed Roman garden.

66. North Leigh (Oxfordshire): this extensive villa is well maintained, with a hypocaust and mosaic under a cover building.

three sides and a central gatehouse. The hypocaust and mosaic are visible through a window. Extensive outbuildings are known from aerial photography.

Orpington (Crofton), Crofton Road, Orpington, Kent BR6 8AF (TQ 454659). *The site is on the A232 Crofton Road, Orpington, near the railway station and the Civic Halls. Car parking is usually possible nearby. The site is administered by the Borough of Bromley and has limited opening hours; a preliminary enquiry is advised. Telephone: 020 8462 4737. Website: www.bromley.gov.uk*

Although the villa (figure 67) was truncated by the railway station and later buildings, ten of its rooms were saved and in 1993 displayed under a cover building. An apparently late villa, it survived well into the fourth century.

Orton Longueville, Cambridgeshire (TL 149977). *Turn off the A605 3 km (2 miles) east of the junction with the A1 near Water Newton and 5 km (3 miles) west of Peterborough. Follow the signs to Nene Park Ferry Meadows. The Roman buildings are in the recreation grounds near the car park.*

This was one of the 'industrial' villas that apparently owed their prosperity to the Castor pottery kilns. Here the main house is still undiscovered, but a typical aisled building of the third century is marked out on the site. There is also a well and a possible temple site, with part of a military ditch.

Rockbourne, Fordingbridge, Hampshire SP6 3PG (SU 120170). *The villa is in West Park, 5 km (3 miles) north-west of Fordingbridge, on the south side of a minor road to Rockbourne. Leave Fordingbridge by the B3078 in the direction of Cranborne and turn right after 2.5 km (1¹/₂ miles). The site is in the care of Hampshire County Council and is open daily, April to October. Telephone: 01725 518541. Website: www.hants.gov.uk*

This extensive courtyard villa is marked out and conserved, including a unique hypocaust, a corn-drier and two mosaics. In the centre of the villa lie its origins, a

67. Orpington (Crofton) (Kent): the shepherd has now fled and this Arcadian landscape is part of an outer London suburb. But the villa has been rediscovered and is well worth a visit. (W. Williams and Kent Archaeological Rescue Unit)

68. In this painting of the Rockbourne villa (Hampshire) the residential quarters and the baths are in the foreground, with the garden beyond. No evidence for a formal gatehouse has been found. North is at the bottom. (Michael Codd and Hampshire County Council)

simple masonry strip building of the first century and, below that, an earlier Iron Age circular hut. The former site museum, once a veritable treasure-house, is now a display area with a few exhibits (figure 68).

Upton Park, Dorset (SY 977938). *The site is in Upton Country Park, signposted from the roundabout at the junction of the A350 and the A3049 and a short distance from Poole. The Country Park is open daily but the replica Romano-British house is not generally open. Serious visitors can obtain a key from the wardens, but it is best to arrange a visit in advance. Telephone: 01202 672625.*

The Upton Romano-British Farm was launched in 1985 as an experimental project linked to the study of the salt-working and pottery industries in Poole Harbour. The original of this replica was excavated at Ower, near Upton, and was sponsored by Poole Museums. It represents the most basic type of cottage-house, particularly in the first century AD. The project was genuinely experimental, using authentic technology and with defined research objectives. Sadly, the farm is now closed and the building is used only for schools and occasional events.

Welwyn (Dicket Mead), Welwyn Bypass, Welwyn, Hertfordshire AL6 9NX (TL 235158). *Opposite the so-called 'villa' at the Clock Motel off the Old Welwyn bypass, a steel-lined tunnel leads under the A1(M) motorway. Inside the tunnel are conserved the bath-house and a display of the villa. Open regularly. Telephone: 01707 271362. Website: www.hertsmuseums.org.uk*

This villa apparently consisted of four buildings, one of which contained the small but exceptionally well-preserved bath-house that can be visited. A late creation of the early third century, the baths lasted for little more than a hundred years before demolition. The Dicket Mead villa is less than 500 metres (550 yards) from the more substantial Lockleys villa (figure 13), although the latter is not visible. This estate comprised at least two villas, presumably in some tenurial relationship, four cemeteries, a roadside settlement and a small canal that served the river Mimram.

Other sites

Several other villas can be visited (often with difficulty) but might prove disappointing to the average visitor. Nevertheless, neglected sites can be tidied up and unexpectedly made accessible; so we list these too. They include: Carisbrooke (Isle of Wight, SZ 486877); Itchen Abbas (Hampshire, SU 528348); Spoonley Wood (Gloucestershire, SP 045257); Titsey Park (Surrey, TQ 405546); Wadfield (Gloucestershire, SP 024261); and, in Wales, Llantwit Major (Glamorgan, SS 959699), and Whitton (Glamorgan, ST 081713). The 'villa' at Butser Ancient Farm (Hampshire, SU 719165), was created in 2002–3 for a television series and is to be used for educational purposes. The 'villa' at Colliton Park (Dorchester, SY 693997), is strictly a town-house of Roman Dorchester but is an open site and (though in 2004 the cover building was closed) is worth a visit. The actual villa at Piddington (Northamptonshire, SP 795545), is not visible but has generated a small museum and research centre nearby. At Woodchester (Gloucestershire, SO 838032), the most famous villa mosaic in Britain is marked by an information plaque.

Index